ROAD SHOW

Road Show

Music and Lyrics by
Stephen Sondheim

Book by
John Weidman

THEATRE COMMUNICATIONS GROUP
NEW YORK
2009

Road Show is published by Theatre Communications Group, Inc., 520 Eighth Avenue
24th Floor, New York, NY 10018-4256

This publication is made possible in part with public funds from the New York State
Council on the Arts, a State Agency.

TCG books are exclusively distributed to the book trade by Consortium Book Sales
and Distribution.

LIBRARY OF CONGRESS CATALOGING-IN-PUBLICATION DATA
Sondheim, Stephen.
[Road show. Libretto]
Road show / book by John Weidman ; music and lyrics by Stephen Sondheim.
—1st TCG ed.
p. cm.
ISBN 978-1-55936-341-9
1. Musicals—Librettos. I. Weidman, John, 1946– II. Title.
ML50.S705R63   2009
782.1'40268—dc22   2009038129

Text design and composition by Lisa Govan
Cover design by Barbara de Wilde
Cover photography (clockwise from top left): "El Mirasol," Historical Society of Palm
Beach County; "Times Square in New York City," copyright © Museum of History
and Industry/CORBIS; "Man Singing to Elephant, Miami Beach, Fla.,1924 April 21,"
Claude Matlack Collection, Historical Museum of Southern Florida; "Prospectors in
Tent Settlement at Chilkoot Pass," copyright © Bettmann/CORBIS.

First Edition, December 2009

*With special thanks to Oskar Eustis
and John Doyle*

Road Show

Production History

Road Show was originally commissioned by Max Woodward and Larry Wilker of the John F. Kennedy Center for the Performing Arts. *Wise Guys*, an earlier version of *Road Show*, was first presented by New York Theatre Workshop in New York City (James C. Nicola, Artistic Director; Jo Beddoe, Managing Director). The workshop production opened on October 29, 1999, under the direction of Sam Mendes. The set design was by Mark Thompson, the costume design was by Santo Loquasto, the lighting design was by Peggy Eisenhauer and Jules Fisher, the sound design was by Jonathan Deans, the choreography was by Jonathan Butterell, the orchestrations were by Jonathan Tunick, the music supervision was by Paul Gemignani and the musical direction was by Ted Sperling. The stage manager was Bonnie Panson. The cast was:

ADDISON MIZNER	Nathan Lane
WILSON MIZNER	Victor Garber
MAMA MIZNER	Candy Buckley
PAPA MIZNER	William Parry
HOLLIS BESSEMER	Michael C. Hall
ENSEMBLE	Brooks Ashmanskas, Jessica Boevers, Kevin Chamberlin, Christopher Fitzgerald, Jessica Molasky, Nancy Opel, Clarke Thorell, Lauren Ward, Ray Wills

Bounce, a revised version of *Wise Guys*, was originally produced by the Goodman Theatre in Chicago (Robert Falls, Artistic Director; Roche Schulfer, Executive Director). The production opened on June 30, 2003, under the direction of Harold Prince. The set design was by Eugene Lee, the costume design was by Miguel Angel Huidor, the lighting design was by Howell Binkley, the sound design was by Duncan Robert Edwards, the choreography was by Michael Arnold, the orchestrations were by Jonathan Tunick and the musical direction was by David Caddick. The stage manager was Rolando Linares and the production stage manager was Alden Vasquez. The cast was:

ADDISON MIZNER	Richard Kind
WILSON MIZNER	Howard McGillin
MAMA MIZNER	Jane Powell
PAPA MIZNER	Herndon Lackey
HOLLIS BESSEMER	Gavin Creel
NELLIE	Michele Pawk
ENSEMBLE	Sean Blake, Marilynn Bogetich, Tom Daugherty, Jeff Dumas, Deanna Dunagan, Nicole Grothues, Rick Hilsabeck, Jeff Parker, Harriet Nzinga Plumpp, Jenny Powers, Craig Ramsay, Jacquelyn Ritz, Fred Zimmerman

The world premiere of *Road Show* was produced by The Public Theater in New York City (Oskar Eustis, Artistic Director; Andrew D. Hamingson, Executive Director). The production opened on October 28, 2008, under the direction of John Doyle. The set design was by John Doyle, the costume design was by Ann Hould-Ward, the lighting design was by Jane Cox, the sound design was by Dan Moses Schreier, the orchestrations were by Jonathan Tunick and the musical direction was by Mary-Mitchell Campbell. The production stage manager was James Latus. The cast was:

ADDISON MIZNER	Alexander Gemignani
WILSON MIZNER	Michael Cerveris
MAMA MIZNER	Alma Cuervo
PAPA MIZNER	William Parry
HOLLIS BESSEMER	Claybourne Elder
ENSEMBLE	Aisha de Haas, Colleen Fitzpatrick, Mylinda Hull, Mel Johnson, Jr., Orville Mendoza, Anne L. Nathan, Matthew Stocke, William Youmans, Kristine Zbornik
SWINGS	David Garry, Katrina Yaukey

CHARACTERS

ADDISON MIZNER
WILSON MIZNER, his brother
MAMA MIZNER, their mother
PAPA MIZNER, their father
HOLLIS BESSEMER, Addison's boyfriend and business partner
ENSEMBLE

SETTING

America, 1890s through 1930s.

Authors' Note

Addison and Wilson Mizner were born within a year and a half of each other in the early 1870s in Benicia, California. During the course of their long, colorful and often chaotic lives, they crisscrossed the country—sometimes separately, sometimes together—trying their hands at a dizzying array of different enterprises and pursuits, from prospecting for gold in the Yukon to promoting a utopian real-estate venture during the Florida land boom. Addison died in Palm Beach in 1933, leaving behind a handful of uniquely designed Mizner houses. Wilson died within weeks of him, in Hollywood. *Road Show* is the story of their lives—or at any rate, our version of it.

—*Stephen Sondheim and John Weidman*

Musical Numbers

Waste	*The Company*
It's in Your Hands Now	*Papa*
Gold!	*Prospector, Mama, Wilson, Addison and The Company*
Brotherly Love	*Wilson and Addison*
The Game	*Poker Players, Wilson, Addison and The Company*
Addison's Trip	*Addison and The Company*
That Was a Year	*Wilson, Ketchel, Mrs. Yerkes, Armstrong, Jockey and The Company*
Isn't He Something!	*Mama*
Land Boom!	*Real-Estate Agent*
Talent	*Hollis*
You	*Addison, Hollis, The Stotesburys, Mrs. Trumbauer, The Cosdens, The Wanamakers, Mr. Dupont, Mrs. Phipps*
The Best Thing That Ever Has Happened	*Hollis and Addison*
The Game (Reprise)	*Wilson*
Addison's City	*Hollis, Wilson, Addison and The Company*
Boca Raton	*Boca Girl and The Company*
Get Out / Go	*Wilson and Addison*
Finale	*Wlson, Addison, Papa and The Company*

Addison Mizner lies in a bed. He is surrounded by an eclectic pyramid of trunks, old furniture and packing crates.

A WOMAN: Mr. Mizner. There's a gentleman to see you.

(*Addison leans forward expectantly, then falls back on the pillows, dead. The door of a packing crate falls open, revealing Wilson Mizner. Lights up on people distributed around the crates.*)

A MAN:
        Think that he's dead?

ANOTHER MAN:
        Has been for years.

A WOMAN:
        God, what a waste.

A MAN:
        Genius, they said.

A WOMAN:
>Opened frontiers.

ANOTHER WOMAN:
>Really, such a waste.

ANOTHER WOMAN:
>All of that style—

A MAN:
>All that flair—

ANOTHER MAN:
>All that guile—

ANOTHER MAN:
>Now, let's be fair.
>He had a real spark.

ANOTHER MAN:
>Made a mark.

A WOMAN:
>Instantly erased.

A MAN:
>Could have been rich.

A WOMAN:
>Could have lost weight.

A MAN:
>God, what a waist.

ADDISON: Excuse me . . .

TWO MEN:

> Son of a bitch
> Could have been great.

A WOMAN AND A MAN:

> Now he's just disgraced.

ADDISON: Ex*cuse* me?—

A WOMAN:

> Such an ascent—

A MAN:

> Such a fall—

ANOTHER MAN:

> Such a nice gent—

THE COMPANY:

> He had it all.
> How could he miss,
> Finish like this?
> Waste.

A MAN:

> Remember me?
> I'm the one that you bought the plantation from.
> Boy, what a waste.
> That was a waste . . .

A WOMAN:

> *(Overlapping:)*
> Remember me?
> I'm the one with the house you designed—
> What a waste, what a terrible waste,
> What a waste . . .

A MAN:

(Overlapping:)
Remember me?
I'm the one that you baited the suckers with.
Waste.
Waste of your money and waste of my time.
Remember that? Remember that?
What a waste, what an asinine waste . . .

TWO WOMEN:

(Overlapping:)
Remember me?
I'm the one that you used in the ads.
Honey, that was a waste,
That was a waste and a half.
Remember that? Remember that?
What a waste, what a silly old waste . . .

A MAN:

(Overlapping:)
Remember me?
I'm the one with the fireworks business—
A waste if I ever saw waste.
And, believe me, I recognize waste
When I come across waste . . .

ANOTHER MAN:

(Overlapping:)
You come into my office
And buy all those pineapples.
Nothing but waste.
I mean, talk about waste.
That was a waste, no, a waste and a half . . .

A WOMAN:

> *(Overlapping:)*
> Not to mention
> The door you forgot to include
> And the stairs that went nowhere.
> *There* was a waste,
> There was a terrible waste . . .

A MAN:

> *(Overlapping:)*
> Remember me?
> I'm the one with the Klondike saloon.
> What a waste, what a god-awful waste.
> I mean, that was a waste . . .

A WOMAN:

> *(Overlapping:)*
> Remember me?
> I'm the one that you promised a mansion to . . .

HANDSOME YOUNG MAN:

> Remember me?
> I'm the one that you fucked.

(Addison blinks at him, stunned.)

ALL:

> Such a good start,
> Such a bad end—
> Leaves a bad taste.

HANDSOME YOUNG MAN:

> I'm the one that you fucked.

(Pause.)

ALL:

> Squandered his art,
> Cheated his friend—
> All of it a waste.

ADDISON: You're the one that I loved.

THREE MEN:

> Destined to fail—

TWO WOMEN:

> Poor old guy.

GROUP 1:

> Losing the trail—

GROUP 2:

> And you know why.

WILSON:

> Everybody shoo!
> I said shoo!
> I mean you . . . shoo!

> *(Opening his arms)* A hug for your old brother? *(Climbing into bed beside Addison)*

> Wasting your time,
> Listening to them—
> That was the waste.

ADDISON: Willie—

WILSON:

> What was your crime?
> You were a gem,
> They were strictly paste.

ADDISON: Willie, listen to me—

WILSON:

> So it got rough,
> Why the guilt?
> Look at the stuff
> That you built.
> So you got burned.
> Look what you've learned!—

ADDISON: You know what I learned, Willie? I learned that the only thing wrong with my life was you. You conniving son of a bitch! *(He swats Wilson)*

WILSON *(Swatting him back)*: Hey, cut it out!

ADDISON *(Another swat)*: You ruined me!

WILSON *(Another swat)*: You ruined yourself!

ADDISON *(Another swat)*: Say it! *You ruined me!*

WILSON: Did not!

ADDISON: Did so!

WILSON: Did not!

ADDISON: Did so!

> *(They fight on the bed, the tussle becoming more and more childlike.)*

WILSON AND ADDISON:

> Mama . . . Mama . . . *Mama!*

(Mama Mizner appears.)

MAMA: Addison! Wilson! Children, stop that this instant!

WILSON: He started it!

ADDISON: I started a lot of things! Who finished 'em?!

WILSON: Blames everybody but himself!

ADDISON: Not everybody!

MAMA: I said, that's *enough*, boys!

(They stop fighting.)

This is no time for squabbling. Your papa's been asking for you.

(The bed is now occupied by Papa Mizner.)

WILSON: Sorry, Mama. How is he?
MAMA: The doctor says it's time now.
ADDISON: Poor Papa.
PAPA: Willie? Addie? Is that you, boys?
WILSON: We're here, Papa.
PAPA: Good, good. Come close, boys. Listen. Boys, your forefathers were given a great gift. A New World, pristine and unspoiled, in which anything was possible. It was my generation's task to make of that New World a nation. Now, with the dawning of a new century, your work begins. The work of determining what type of nation we shall be. Behind you, at your backs, the boundless riches of a mighty land. Before you, unfolding at your feet . . .

> There's a road straight ahead,
> There's a century beginning.
> There's a land of opportunity and more.
> It's in your hands now.
>
> There are dreams to be fed,
> There's a world that's worth the winning,
> There's a legacy of riches that's in store.
>
> Now it's up to you,
> And you'll see it through
> If you stay on track
> And you don't look back.
> It's in your hands now.
> Time to start your journey now.

Never falter, never rest
Until you know
You've achieved the very best
That you can be,
Never pausing in your quest
For something better just around the corner.

Up to you to set the course
Of where we'll go,
With the limitless resources
You can plumb.
Keep your eyes on what's afar,
Not on what we are,
But what we can become!

Follow on where we've led,
Make the past an underpinning
For the future, for the road you must explore.
As the road extends,
It gets rough as it ascends,
And it often bends,
But it never, ever ends.
It will take you anywhere you want,
If you know where you're going.

It's in your hands now, boys,
Make of it what you will, but make me proud—
Make me proud. Make me . . .

(Papa falls back on the pillow, dead.)

ADDISON: What do we do now, Mama?
MAMA: That's up to you, boys. You're the men of the family now.
WILSON: Mama's right, we are.
MAMA: Which means you need to know exactly how things stand.
   Your papa was ill for a very long time, boys. Caring for him
   was expensive.

WILSON: You don't mean we're *poor*?

MAMA: I mean when opportunity knocks, we need to answer.

ADDISON: It's just like Papa said. Somewhere out there, there's a road. A road for *us*.

WILSON: The question is, how do we find it?

(A Prospector appears.)

PROSPECTOR:
> Gold!
> Bet your little titty, boy!

MAMA:
> Gold!

PROSPECTOR:
> Gold!
> Nuggets this thick!

MAMA:
> Gold!

PROSPECTOR:
> Gold!
> Go to Dawson City, boy—
> It isn't very pretty,
> But it's get rich quick!
>
> Found me a mother lode,
> Warn't no trick!
> Wanna find another lode?
> Dig in any mountain,
> Pan in any crick!
> Grab yourself a bucket
> And a shovel and a pick
> And with a little bit of luck it
> Means you . . .

THE COMPANY:
> Get rich quick! . . .

MAMA *(As if quoting a newspaper)*: "GOLD RUSH IN THE YUKON!"
WILSON: "RICHEST STRIKE SINCE SUTTER'S MILL!"
ADDISON: Boy, oh, boy, if Papa was alive—
MAMA: He isn't.
WILSON: Let's go!
ADDISON: Where? To *Alaska*?

MAMA:
> Haven't you been listening?
> Gold,
> Sitting there and glistening!
> Gold just
> Lying around!
> Gold dust
> Glittering and littering the goddamn ground!

ADDISON: But in *Alaska*? Way up in *Alaska*?

WILSON:
> Oh, come on, Addie,
> The two of us together!—
> What fun!

ADDISON: But what about Mama? We can't just *leave* her here.
MAMA: Why not?!

WILSON:
> You and me against the world, Addie,
> You and me against the world!
> You and me together,
> Weathering the weather,
> Fording the crevasses—

ADDISON:
> Freezing off our asses—

WILSON:
> We'll never make our fortune
> Just by sitting on the porch 'n'
> Looking wistful,
> When there are nuggets by the fistful . . .

MAMA: Nuggets by the fistful!—

> Time to leave the nest,
> Time to venture forth.

WILSON AND MAMA:
> Can't go further west,
> Might as well go north,
> Where there's all that—

ADDISON: Cold.

WILSON AND MAMA:
> Gold!

ADDISON: I don't know . . .

MAMA:
> "Grab the opportunity!"

ADDISON: How would we even get there?

MAMA:
> That's what Papa said.

ADDISON: The whole thing might be over by the time—

MAMA:

> "Grab the opportunity
> And take the road ahead!"

ADDISON: I don't think he meant *any* oppor—

MAMA:

> Never be content with what you are,
> But think of what you can become!

WILSON: Listen to Mama. She knows best.

> Not to grab the chance,
> Wouldn't that be dumb?

MAMA:

> Papa said to grab,
> And the world's your plum!

ADDISON: Did he? I suppose so, in a way . . .
MAMA: Your papa said you'd find your road and here it is.
WILSON: The road to riches!

THE COMPANY:

> Gold!

ADDISON: I'm not sure he was talking about riches, Willie—

THE COMPANY:

> Gold!!

WILSON: Not *only* riches! Enterprise! *Adventure!*

THE COMPANY:

> Gold! Gold!!

ADDISON: Alaska . . .
WILSON: Okay. If you won't go—then how about you?
MAMA: Wait while I go get my shawl!
ADDISON: Hey!

THE COMPANY:
    Gold!

WILSON: Joke! I can't go without you. We're a team!

THE COMPANY:
    Gold!

ADDISON: A team. We would be, wouldn't we?

THE COMPANY:
    Gold! Gold!

WILSON: You bet we would—
ADDISON: Okay, we'll do it! Me and you!

WILSON:
        A century's beginning—
        Gold will make it tick!
        A century of enterprise
        For you and me to lick!
        Papa made it clear,
        The opportunity is here,
        And if to be a pioneer
        Means that you get rich quick,
        So—?

MAMA:
        A century's beginning,
        Gold will make it tick!
        A century of enterprise

For both of you to lick!
That's what Papa meant—you're
Going off on an adventure!
Just a shovel and a tent, you're
Off and entering the century—

WILSON:

(Overlapping:)
You and me against
The world, Addie!
You and me against
The world!
You and me together,
Weathering the weather—

ADDISON:

(Overlapping:)
A shovel and a tent,
We're off and entering the century—

ADDISON, MAMA AND WILSON:

You and me (he)
Against the world, Addie (Willie)!
You and me (he)
Against the world!
You and me (he) together,
Weathering the weather
As we're (you're) entering the century
Of get rich quick!

THE COMPANY:

(Simultaneously with Addison, Mama and Wilson:)
The century's beginning,
Gold will make it tick!
Dig in any mountain, pan in any crick.
All you need's a bucket and a shovel and a pick

And with a little bit of luck it
Means you get rich quick!
Get rich quick! Get rich quick!
Get—!

ALL *(Except Mama and Addison)*:
Rich—

ALL:

Quick!
Gold!

(Alaska. Addison and Wilson lie in sleeping bags. The wind howls.)

WILSON: Jesus, it's cold . . . Are you awake? . . . Are you awake?

ADDISON: I am now, Willie.

WILSON: Then pass me the canteen, will you? I can't reach it without getting out of my sleeping— Oh, shit.

ADDISON: What's the matter?

WILSON: What's the matter? You want to know what's the matter?

ADDISON: Willie—

WILSON: Every hour of every day for the past three months I have been either freezing cold or soaking wet or both! For three months I have worked half a dozen different claims, digging great big bottomless holes which have produced exactly nothing! And my sleeping bag, which has been soggy since the blizzard last week, just split up the middle! That, for starters, is what's the matter!

ADDISON: You can sleep in my bag if you want.

WILSON: And where are you going to sleep?

ADDISON: We could share it.

WILSON: That's going to be kind of a tight squeeze, Addie.

ADDISON: You're right. Bad idea.

WILSON: What the hell—

(Wilson dashes through the howling wind and slides into Addison's sleeping bag. He and Addison are squeezed up against each other, spoon style, with Addison behind Wilson. Pause. Wilson tries to warm himself.)

ADDISON: You know what this reminds me of?
WILSON: No. What?

ADDISON:
    Remember when I was in bed with the mumps
    And had to stay in New Year's Eve?

WILSON: Frankly, no.

ADDISON:
    Remember how I was so down in the dumps
    When everyone started to leave?—

WILSON:
    Jesus, it's cold!

ADDISON:
    Are you sorry we came, Willie?
    You sorry we came?

WILSON: Yes. No. Go to sleep.

ADDISON:
    At midnight, with everyone down at the lake
    To take in the fireworks show—

WILSON *(Remembering)*: Oh, yeah.

ADDISON:
    I cried till I fell half asleep by mistake—

WILSON:

> And I snuck upstairs and I shook you awake—

ADDISON:

> And you bundled me up in a couple of quilts
> And you carried me up all the way to the roof—

WILSON:

> *(Simultaneously with Addison, above:)*
> Up all the way to the roof—

(Wind rises.)

ADDISON:

> And that slippery patch!—

WILSON:

> Yeah, we nearly got killed!—

ADDISON:

> But we got to see everything!

WILSON:

> *(Simultaneously with Addison, above:)*
> But we got to see every—
> Remember the whizbangs—?

(The wind howls, drowning them out as they tumble over each other in reminiscences, singing in pantomime. As the wind dies down:)

We had lots of good times . . .

(They chuckle in memory. Pause.)

26

ADDISON:

> We slept there till dawn,
> All wrapped up in those quilts . . .

WILSON:

> Boy, Mama was madder than hell . . .

(They snicker. Pause.)

ADDISON:

> You always looked out for me, no matter what . . .

WILSON:

> Just brotherly love, brother, brotherly love—
> *(Sniffs)*
> Jesus, I smell.

ADDISON:

> I'm not sorry I came, Willie,
> Just as long as you're here . . .

(The wind rises as the music fades. Addison looks suddenly uneasy. He pivots away nervously so that he and Wilson are back to back.)

WILSON: Turn around, will you?
ADDISON: I'm fine like this.
WILSON: Maybe you are, but I can't breathe. Turn around.
ADDISON: I'm comfortable this way.
WILSON: For Christ's sakes—
ADDISON: No!
WILSON: *Fine! Swell! Take the whole thing!*

(Wilson throws himself out of the sleeping bag.)

ADDISON: What are you doing?

WILSON: We need supplies. I'm going back to Skagway. I'll pick them up along with a new sleeping bag and I'll be back tomorrow night.

ADDISON: I'll go with you.

WILSON: You'll stay here and work the claim. That's why we got all excited about coming up here, remember?

ADDISON: Okay, but hurry, all right?

(A ramshackle saloon. Three Poker Players playing cards. They eye Wilson as he enters.)

POKER PLAYERS 1–3:
 Gold . . .

POKER PLAYER 1:
 Got us a beginner, boys—

POKER PLAYERS 1–3:
 Gold . . .

POKER PLAYER 1:
 Fresh off the ground.

POKER PLAYERS 1–3:
 Gold! Gold!

POKER PLAYER 1:
 This one is a winner, boys—

POKER PLAYER 3:
 Pluck it from a mountain
 Or pluck it from a hick—

POKER PLAYER 2:
 When you see a chance, you pluck it
 Off of someone who has struck it—

POKER PLAYER 3:
> You don't have to have a bucket
> Or a shovel or a pick—

POKER PLAYER 1:
> All you really need is luck or
> An accommodating sucker
> Who imagines that he's slick—

POKER PLAYERS 1–3:
> And who doesn't know he's thick—

POKER PLAYER 1:
> And it—

> —looks like you've been roughin' it out there for quite some time, fella.

WILSON: Three months—

POKER PLAYER 1: Three months! Mickey, pour this boy a drink!

WILSON: Thanks, but I don't—

POKER PLAYER 1 *(Brandishing cards)*: Why don't you take a load off and relax?

WILSON: Poker? Oh, no thanks. I play a little rummy sometimes, that's about it. Besides, my brother's waiting for me—

POKER PLAYER 1: The game is five-card stud. One-eyed jacks and deuces wild.

WILSON *(Half a beat)*: One-eyed jacks? What are one-eyed jacks? . . .

(Back at the claim, Addison is swinging a pickax.)

THE COMPANY:
> Gold!

ADDISON:
> Grab the opportunity . . .

29

THE COMPANY:
> Gold!

ADDISON:
> Two musketeers . . .

THE COMPANY:
> Gold!

ADDISON:
> Part of a community
> Of pioneers!
> "Oh, come on, Addie,
> The two of us together,
> What fun!"—
> Fun . . .
> I'm straining every sinew,
> Getting blisters and continually—
> *(Sneezes)*
> Sneezing,
> Wolves are howling and it's freezing,
> Where's the goddamn gold?!
> This is really silly—gold!
> And where the hell is Willie?

(He hits a rock with his pickax.)

Ow!

> Maybe this is not the road, Papa,
> Maybe not the road for me.
> Maybe it's for Willie —
> Yes, I know I'm being silly,
> But it isn't what I want.
> I don't think it's what I want.
> At the moment all I want
> Is Willie . . .

(Back at the saloon, where Wilson has joined the game.)

POKER PLAYER 1: I'll see your two-fifty and I'll raise you three thousand. Assuming, of course, you *got* three thousand.

WILSON *(Counting his chips)*: Two thousand one hundred and eighty-five.

POKER PLAYER 1: Which I'm afraid means that you forfeit the—

(Addison enters.)

ADDISON: There you are!

WILSON: Addie!

ADDISON: Don't "Addie" me! Where the hell have you been for the last three weeks?!

WILSON: Three weeks! It hasn't been—

ADDISON: Do you know what it was like for me out there?! Alone?! Do you know what I had to live with?! Blizzards! Frostbite! Wolves! And for what?! For what?! *(Grins, draws Wilson aside, producing a large nugget)* As it turns out, for this: We found it, Willie! It's all ours! All we have to do is dig it up!

WILSON: Jesus, would you look at that? You got the claim with you?

ADDISON: Of course I've got the claim! Boy, oh, boy, wait'll Mama sees—

WILSON: Hang on. Boys, this is my brother Addison and he just dug up *this* nugget in the middle of *this* claim. Now we can argue about what they're worth, or I can see your three thousand— *(Brandishing the nugget)* And raise you, say, five hundred— *(Brandishing the claim)*

ADDISON: Would you excuse us for a minute? Just one minute . . . *(Drawing Wilson aside)* Willie, what are you doing?! Betting the *claim*?! You can't bet the claim!

WILSON: Addie, listen. We came up here to strike it rich, right? Well, we did. Twice. You out there and me in here!

ADDISON: What are you talking about?!

31

WILSON: How long's it going to take us to dig that gold out of the ground? Three months? Three years? I can dig it out of that guy's pocket in three seconds!

ADDISON: *Willie!*

WILSON:

> Never let a chance go by, Addie,
> Isn't that what Papa meant?
> Now and then you miss one,
> But I guarantee you this one
> Is a winner.
> I'm no longer a beginner!
>
> Addie, take the chance
> Or it disappears!
> Every card you're dealt opens new frontiers—
> Let's be pioneers!

ADDISON: Willie, that claim could be worth a fortune! Why would we *gamble* it?!

WILSON: Why wouldn't we?

ADDISON: Oh God . . .

WILSON:

> The whole thing's nothing more than just a game.
> And, Addie, what I'm good at is the game.
> They said, "Come on in, sucker!"
> Now they're sorry that I came.
> I tell you, kid, there's nothing like the game.
>
> Better than girls, better than booze,
> Beating ace high with a pair of twos.
> Better than snowdrifts in your shoes,
> Even if now and then you lose—

ADDISON: Exactly!

WILSON:

> The thing that really matters is the game.
> It's more than just the winning, it's the game.
> That moment when the card is turned
> And nothing is the same—
> The only thing that matters is the game.
>
> Better than smokes, better than snuff,
> Hooking a sucker just enough,
> Betting your bundle on a bluff—
> Jesus, what a moment!
>
> It's more than just the money that's at stake.
> That's nice, but it's just icing on the cake.
> It's your life every pot,
> Who you are, not what you've got.
> Compared to that, the world seems pretty tame.
> The thing that really matters is the game.
>
> What do you think Papa would say?
> "Boys," he'd say, "Seize the goddamn day!
> This is your chance—"

ADDISON:

> All right, okay!

(Wilson makes the bet, reveals his hand. The Poker Players throw down their cards in a frustrated rage.)

ADDISON: What happened?
POKER PLAYER 1: Heart flush.
POKER PLAYERS 1–3: Your buddy won.
ADDISON: I'd like a drink, please. *(The Bartender starts to pour)* A big one.

(The Bartender turns to face him. It's Papa.)

PAPA: "Go forth and make me proud—"

ADDISON: Oh, Jesus—

PAPA: Games of chance, cheap liquor. What's next? Dancing girls and a roulette wheel?

ADDISON: It was one hand, Papa. And we won.

PAPA: You think so, huh?

(Papa disappears.)

WILSON: Brother, we're in business!

ADDISON: What?

WILSON: Ten thousand dollars!

ADDISON: And the claim. Time to go back and work the claim.

WILSON: Claim's gone. I swapped it for the saloon.

ADDISON: You swapped it *what?*

WILSON: For the saloon. Hey, I *said* we were in business! Sure, the place looks like a dump now. But I'm thinking we'll put in a little stage for dancing girls. Maybe a roulette wheel—

ADDISON: Gimme the money.

WILSON: What?

ADDISON: Give me the money!

(Addison snatches roughly half the cash and heads off.)

WILSON: Where are you going?

ADDISON: Away from you!

(Out front:)

I'm on my way!
Look, Mama, on my own!
I lost my way—
That was just an episode.
I'm on my way,
Off to worlds I've never known—
I'm looking for my road!

34

(Ship's horn.)

> Let Willie stay.
> I mean, Willie's found his niche.
> I have to say,
> We were getting just too entwined.
> But that's okay,
> And so what if I don't get rich?
> I'm on my way to find
> My road!

("Hawaiian" music. Addison arrives in Honolulu and meets a Hawaiian Businessman.)

HAWAIIAN BUSINESSMAN: Aloha, Mr. Mizner. Welcome to Hawaii. And congratulations, you just bought yourself a half share in United Pineapple!

ADDISON: Great!

WILSON *(Outside the scene, observing)*: Unfortunately, the pineapple plantation—

(Crackling flames. Screams . . .)

—just caught on fire—

(Three Hawaiians appear, hawking souvenirs.)

THREE HAWAIIANS:
> Souvenir of your visit to Hawaii . . .
> Souvenir, so the memory will stay in your mind . . .
> Souvenir of the day you say goodbyii . . .
> Souvenir for the girl you left behind . . .
> *(Light glows on Mama)*
> Native spear . . .

ADDISON:
>Just a little setback,
>Mama . . .

THREE HAWAIIANS:
>Buy it here . . .

ADDISON:
>Little setbacks are allowed . . .

THREE HAWAIIANS:
>Souvenir . . .

ADDISON:
>By the time I get back,
>You'll be proud.

(Addison buys souvenirs.)

>I'm on my way,
>Discouraged not at all.
>I'm on my way
>To I don't care where or when.
>A brand-new day
>And a brand-new port of call—
>I'm on my way again!

(Ship's horn.)

>A small delay
>Doesn't shake my confidence.
>I'm on my way
>To discover who I am.
>And on my way
>I've acquired experience,
>Plus a rattan stool from a native hut,

A candle stand made of coconut,
A whatnot made out of god-knows-what—
I'm on my way again!
Hot damn!

("Indian" music. Addison arrives in Bombay and meets an Indian Businessman.)

INDIAN BUSINESSMAN: Congratulations, Mr. Mizner. You have just become a full partner in Bombay's Emporium of Precious Gems.
ADDISON: Great.
WILSON: Unfortunately, the Emporium was just hit—

(Cyclonic winds. Screams . . .)

—by a cyclone—

(Three Indian Souvenir Sellers appear.)

INDIAN 1:
 Sahib like a chair
 With inscription of a swami?

INDIAN 2:
 Something very rare—
 Made for raja, only one of a kind . . .

INDIAN 3:
 How about a pair,
 One for Daddy, one for Mommy?—

INDIANS 1–3:
 Don't you care
 For the girl you left behind?
 (Light glows on Mama again)
 Chandelier . . .

ADDISON:
>I've still got resources, Mama—

INDIANS 1–3:
>For your dear . . .

ADDISON:
>And I'm learning as I go.

INDIANS 1–3:
>Souvenir . . .

ADDISON:
>Failing merely forces
>You to grow.

(Addison buys more souvenirs.)

>I'm on my way,
>At sea but far from wrecked.
>I went astray,
>As who doesn't now and then?
>But on my way
>I've acquired some self-respect,
>Plus an old stone jug
>And a fakir's rug,
>A chandelier that's a bitch to lug
>And a rattan stool and a coconut
>And a whatnot which wasn't worth it, but
>I'm on my way again—
>Again.

("Chinese" music. Addison arrives in Hong Kong and meets an English Businessman.)

ENGLISH BUSINESSMAN: Congratulations, Mr. Mizner! You are now co-owner of Hong Kong's premier fireworks manufactory.

ADDISON: Great.
WILSON: Unfortunately—

(A spectacular explosion. Screams . . . Three Chinese Souvenir Sellers appear.)

CHINESE 1:
   Souvenir—
   Can't go empty-handed!

CHINESE 2:
   Blue veneer—
   Very hard to find . . .

CHINESE 3:
   Gift to cheer
   Missy feeling stranded—

CHINESE 1–3:
   Missy who you left behind!
   (Light glows on Mama again)
   Souvenir . . . souvenir . . .

ADDISON:
   I've half a dozen letters to mail you . . .
   Don't worry, Mama, I won't fail you . . .

(Addison buys more souvenirs.)

   I'm in my way.
   It's a bit disheartening.
   I'm in my way,
   Still I'm doing as I please,
   Facing life's adversities.
   I've got lots of memories—

Plus a Ming tureen
Made of opaline
And a ten-foot scroll
And a lacquered screen
And a chandelier
And a swami's chair
And a sense that worse is to come, but where?—

(Fiery "Latin" music.)

GUATEMALANS:

In Guatemala,
Where everyone feels hot and free . . .
Enjoy your stay in Guatemala,
The land of sensuality . . .

(Addison arrives in Guatemala City and meets a Guatemalan Plantation Owner.)

ADDISON: That's it, that's all the money I've got left. I know you can't guarantee me a sure thing, but—

PLANTATION OWNER: As a matter of fact, Mr. Mizner, that's precisely what I *can* guarantee you. The coffee business in Guatemala is a cartel, controlled by the same wealthy families that control the government. So frankly, unless we have a revolution—

NATIVE 1: *Revolution!*

(Gunshots, Screams . . . Addison grabs his souvenirs and runs for his life.)

ADDISON: This is ridiculous . . . Where am I going? . . . What am I *doing*?

I give up!

Two years, halfway around the world, and what have I got to show for it? Embarrassment! Humiliation! Malaria!—

And a gilded mirror, an iron trunk,
A statue carved by a Spanish monk
And a ton of other assorted junk!

"Boys, be bold!" "Your path is clear!" Ha! The only thing that's clear is that no matter what I try, I make a big, fat fool of myself! I'm sorry, Papa. I know I said I'd make you and Mama proud. I know you said there was a road out there, somewhere, even for me. Well, maybe there is, but I've looked everywhere and, Papa, I can't find it . . .

(He slumps, totally defeated. The Company rearranges his souvenirs.)

No, they all seem out of place . . .

(The Company rearranges them again.)

Now it all looks too compressed . . .
What I need to have is space
That holds crucifixes,
A Bombay chest,
A temple bell
And a condor's nest
And commodes and mirrors and all the rest—
I'll need a hundred rooms!
(Pause. Quietly:)
So I'll make a hundred rooms . . .
(With growing enthusiasm:)
Give the Chinese scroll an entire wall,
The gilded mirror a separate hall,
Build an atrium for the chandelier,
Give the rug a room with some atmosphere,

41

Build a marble niche for the Ming tureen
And a mezzanine for the lacquered screen,
And an archway here and a skylight there
Until everything has a place somewhere—

I'll build a goddamned house!

I'm on my way . . .

(Thunder. The sound of rain. Addison is now in an atelier in Greenwich Village. Wilson appears.)

WILSON: Surprise.
ADDISON: Willie!

(Mama appears.)

MAMA: Hello, dear.
ADDISON: Oh my God—
WILSON: Now *that's* a surprise, huh?
ADDISON: Mama, I don't believe it! Where did you come from?! How did you find me?! I wrote you, both of you. In San Francisco, and Alaska. I thought you were still in Skagway, running that saloon—
WILSON: Won it with a heart flush, lost it with a busted one. Anyway, where does a boy go when all he's got left in the world is frostbite, a pair of ratty longjohns, and a sob story?
MAMA: Home to Mama.
WILSON: Home to Mama! And as it turns out, in the nick of time, too. There she was, living like a hermit, rattling around in that big old empty house. I rattled around with her for a while. No one could track *you* down—
ADDISON: I know, I—
WILSON: So we sold the house and started moving east. Santa Fe.
MAMA: St. Louis.

WILSON: One adventure after another—

MAMA: I told your brother, I said, just once when we check out of a hotel I'd like to take a nice, boring walk right out the front door instead of climbing down the fire escape.

WILSON: And here we are—New York, New York! Now how 'bout you? Last time I saw you, you were running like a thief through six feet of snow with a fistful of my poker winnings.

ADDISON: Yeah. You know, I'm sorry about that, Willie. I guess I just . . . I don't know, I felt like—

WILSON: If you were ever going to find your road you were going to have to do it without me.

ADDISON: Yeah.

WILSON: And did you?

ADDISON: It turns out I've got a talent, Willie. Not for making money, but for making art. I'm going to build things, all kinds of things. I see them all, inside my head. Office buildings, railway stations, concert halls. It's like there's a whole new way America should look and it's all up here, between these ears. See this? *(Indicates an architectural plan)* The American Society of Architects has an annual competition, this year for a "major country residence," and I'm entering. Echoes of Guatemala, a touch of the British Raj, a little bit of everything I picked up while I was traveling. And I've got my first commission. A pool house for a widow out in Oyster Bay. It isn't much, but it pays the bills—well, it almost pays the bills. And most important, it's a start.

MAMA: You must be very pleased, dear.

WILSON: Hell, he's on his way!

(A knock.)

ADDISON: Goodness, I almost forgot. I've got an appointment. My client, Myra Yerkes—

WILSON: Myra Yerkes?

ADDISON: She's come to see my plans. To approve them and to pay me the first half of my fee.

43

WILSON: You don't mean the Myra Yerkes whose husband walked in front of one of his own streetcars and left her fifty million bucks? *That* Myra Yerkes?

ADDISON: Willie, please. The woman's still in mourning.

(Mrs. Yerkes enters.)

MRS. YERKES: Who's he?

ADDISON: I'm sorry? Oh, my brother Wilson, Mrs. Myra Yerkes—

WILSON: Dear lady, please accept my most profound condolences.

ADDISON: And now, for your pleasure, and I hope for your approval, Mrs. Yerkes— *(Revealing a set of plans)* Your new pool house!

WILSON: Forgive me, but I'm curious. A woman of your standing obviously travels with a car and driver, but it appears that you've been forced to walk.

MRS. YERKES: My chauffeur. He shot his big mouth off once too often so I canned him.

WILSON: Despicable. When you're ready to leave, perhaps you'll permit me to put you in a cab.

MRS. YERKES: Let's go.

(They exit. Organ music.)

MINISTER'S VOICE: . . . by the Sovereign State of New York, I now pronounce you man and wife. You may kiss the bride.

(Mrs. Yerkes and Wilson kiss. A bell rings and Stanley Ketchel, a prizefighter, appears.)

MAMA *(In bed, holding a newspaper)*: Addie, look at this! Your brother's in the prizefight business!

WILSON:
    Kid!

KETCHEL:
> Hiya, Willie!

WILSON:
> How you doing?

KETCHEL:
> Just great!

MRS. YERKES:
> Who's that?!

WILSON:
> Stanley Ketchel,
> Fighting Sailor Boy Mackenzie
> For the title.

MRS. YERKES:
> For the title?

WILSON:
> For the middleweight crown.
> We bought his contract
> For a measly fifty thousand.

MRS. YERKES:
> We *did?*

Remind me, when exactly did we buy his—?

KETCHEL: I just wanna say thank you to our Lord and Savior Jesus Christ, to my sainted mother, may she rest in peace, and most of all to the greatest manager a fighter ever had, Willie Mizner!

(The crowd roars.)

Willie had style,
Willie had brass,
Willie said, "Stan, I'm gonna give you some class."
Taught me to dress,
Made me a sport,
Gave me social status and something to snort.

Learned a lot from Willie,
Havin' laughs, gettin' tight,
Coked till we were silly
By the dawn's early light.
Learned so much from Willie
I forgot how to fight,
But oh, what a year,
That was a year!

MRS. YERKES: Next time you go shopping with my dough, let me know, okay?

WILSON:

God, I love this town!
Don't you love this town?
It's got all of these
Opportunities,
Can't afford to turn them down!

Some may not work out.
Some go up the spout,
Plenty more around the corner—
And what's waiting round the corner,
Isn't that what life is all about?

ADDISON (*On the phone*): I know you're busy, Willie, I read the papers. But Mama thought she was going to see you Sunday and she— . . . This Sunday? You're sure? Okay, just as long as you're sure. And don't forget to bring my fee! (*Hangs up*)

MAMA: Addie, you won't believe it! Your brother's written a Broadway play!

(Paul Armstrong, a famous playwright, flamboyantly theatrical, appears.)

ARMSTRONG:
> Willie had wit,
> Willie had brains,
> Willie had contacts in the lower domains.
> Knew how they lived,
> Knew what they'd say.
> That's why I said, "Willie, let's write a play."

> But where the hell was Willie
> Came the time to rewrite?
> Way the hell in Philly,
> Off promoting some fight.
> Half a play with Willie
> Closes opening night,
> But oh, what a year!
> That was a year!

MRS. YERKES: You're saying I *invested* in this play?

WILSON:
> God, I love it here!
> Don't you love it here?

MRS. YERKES: That I invested *fifteen thousand bucks* in this play?

WILSON:
> Every place you look
> Is an open book,
> Every street a new frontier!
> If you sizzle, swell.

47

If you fizzle—well,
Nothing fails for long.
If it doesn't fly, it doesn't,
And it's time to sing another song!

CHORINES, KETCHEL AND ARMSTRONG:
Broadway Willie,
Prince of bon vivants—
Everybody wants
Broadway Willie Mizner!

Knocks 'em silly,
Lowlifes and Duponts,
Cops and debutantes . . .

ADDISON *(On the phone again)*: You didn't make it last Sunday or the Sunday before, Willie, what makes you think you're going to make it— . . . Fine, I'll tell her. And Willie, please, I need that fee! *(Hangs up)*
MAMA: Look at this picture, dear! Your brother kissing a racehorse!

(A Jockey in handcuffs.)

JOCKEY:
Willie and me, we had a run,
Doin' some things we shouldn't of done,
Till we get rumbled for this race we try to fix.
Willie says, "Kid, I'm your support.
Let me explain things to the court."
So he explains and beats the rap
And I get sent up for six.

ARMSTRONG:
Now I write a show,
It doesn't get on . . .

KETCHEL:
> Offer me some dough,
> I dive like a swan . . .

JOCKEY:
> Once I was a pro,
> And now I'm a con.
> But oh, what a year!

KETCHEL AND ARMSTRONG:
> That was a year!

WILSON:
> From the mayor to the cop on the beat,
> Who's the only guy they all want to meet?
> Who's the man they call the King of the Street?

THE COMPANY:
> Good Time Willie Mizner!
> When you write about New Yorkers of note,
> Who's the wittiest by popular vote,
> Always ready with a quip or a quote?

WILSON: Be nice to the people you meet on the way up, 'cause they're the same people you're gonna meet on the way down.

THE COMPANY:
> Night club fillies,
> Writers, racketeers,
> Everybody cheers
> Good Time Willie Mizner!
> Ziegfeld lilies,
> Pimps and financiers—

ADDISON *(Back on the phone)*: What fee? The fee for the pool house, Willie! *That's* what fee!

MRS. YERKES:
> Willie had style.
> Willie had gall.
> Willie had ladies round the block and down the hall.
> Perfect in looks,
> Perfect at sex,
> Not so goddamn perfect at forging my checks.

KETCHEL:
> Sure, I lost the crown, but I made lots of green . . .

ARMSTRONG:
> Sure, he took his time, but we wrote a great scene . . .

JOCKEY:
> I was voted "biggest wit" in cell block eighteen . . .

MRS. YERKES, KETCHEL AND ARMSTRONG:
> Thanks to Willie Mizner,
> Nimble Willie Mizner—

KETCHEL:
> Sharp as a hawk—

ARMSTRONG:
> Cock of the walk—

MRS. YERKES: You're telling me . . .

JOCKEY:
> King of Noo Yawk!

THE COMPANY:
> Stick around with Willie, you run out of luck.
> Stick around with Willie, you feel like a cluck.

Stick around with Willie, you're gonna get stuck,
But you'll get a year!—

JOCKEY:

Maybe ten to twenty—

THE COMPANY:

You'll have a year!—

MRS. YERKES:

One was more than plenty!—

THE COMPANY:

You'll have the time of your life!

MRS. YERKES:

I had the time of my life!

WILSON:

God, I love this town!

THE COMPANY:

Broadway Willie,
King of New York!

(Mama, tucked up in the bed in Addison's studio. A tray lies on her lap with dinner on it and the newspapers. Beside the bed, Addison's drafting table.)

ADDISON: Okay, you've got your cutlet, your parsleyed potatoes, and your green beans. Here's the papers. And don't forget what Dr. Stanton told you about getting out of bed.

MAMA: Those are your plans, aren't they? For your pool house? That means you're going to see Wilson.

ADDISON: If he won't come to see me, I'm damn well going to go see him.

MAMA: Well, I should think you would. And you make sure you get your fee this time, too.

ADDISON: You bet I will. Anything else?

MAMA: Yes. You tell your brother I want to know when they're going to run a story about him visiting his poor old shut-in of a mother.

ADDISON: We may not live the high life like Willie does, but I think the two of us are doing fine. And you know what I'll bet? I'll bet he's going to stop by for a visit any day now.

MAMA: You know what I'll bet? I'll bet you're going to lose that bet.

> Never comes to see me,
> Hardly ever calls.
> When he sends me letters,
> They're just two-line scrawls.
> Isn't he something!

ADDISON: Something—?

MAMA:

> Things he says out loud I wouldn't dare,
> Or I'd have to hide.
> Skates along through life without a care
> Or a shred of pride,
> But look at him glide!
> Isn't he something?
> See how he glides.
>
> He's having the time of his life,
> Life filled to the brim.
> And I've had the time of my life,
> Living through him.
>
> Some men are tender souls
> With worthy goals
> They keep fulfilling.

Some men ignore the rules,
Are rogues and fools,
And thrilling.

Honey,
If he had the slightest sense of shame,
It would be a shame.
And isn't he shameless?
Doesn't he glide?
Isn't he something!

I've been a very lucky woman, Addie. To have one son who's
thrilled me and excited me. And another one I knew would
care for me and make me comfortable no matter what.

Carelessness and being free of care,
Aren't they the same?
Some men live to be good,
Some men live to be bad,
Some men live just to sparkle.
And doesn't he sparkle?
See how he glides!
Isn't he something!

(Mama falls back against the pillows, dead.)

ADDISON: Mama . . . ?

(Wilson appears.)

WILSON: Prodigal Kid Makes Comeback!
ADDISON: *Willie—*

(Addison jumps up and pivots the bed away from Wilson.)

WILSON: Hel-*lo*, Addie! And Hel-*lo*, Mama! Sorry. Bad time?

ADDISON: No, no. I'm just . . . You took me by surprise, that's all. Long time no see, you know?

WILSON: Hey, do I ever! I'll tell you, pal, I love this town, but it's a full-time job.

ADDISON: I can imagine. Mama's been keeping track of your adventures in the papers.

WILSON: Truths! Truths! Nothing but truths! How is she?

ADDISON: How are *you*? How's Myra?

WILSON: Myra? Well, I'm guessing, but I'd say she's better than she was before she threw me out.

ADDISON: She threw you out?

WILSON: Like yesterday's papers.

ADDISON: I'm sorry.

WILSON: Yeah? I'm not. Face to the future, Brother! Good-bye to all that!

ADDISON: And all that includes the pool house, I guess.

WILSON: The pool house? . . . Oh, the *pool* house. Hey, you can stop wasting your time on that crap. Build what *you* want. Be an artist! That's what you *said* you were. Well, now's your chance to stop kissing up to rich widows and prove it!

ADDISON: Good advice. Thanks.

WILSON: I had a thought coming over here. I've got no present plans, no place I have to be. How 'bout if I moved in with you and Mama for a while? Give us a chance to catch up, swap a yarn or two about the Yukon. What d'you say?

ADDISON: I think Mama would like that.

WILSON: Would she? I haven't been around much. She isn't sore at me, is she?

ADDISON: At *you*? Nothing you could do could make her sore at you, you know that.

WILSON: Yeah, I guess I do.

(Addison turns the bed, revealing Mama.)

Mama! . . . She's asleep.

ADDISON: It's okay. Wake her up.

WILSON: No, no—

ADDISON: Go on. Surprise her with a kiss.

WILSON: Like sleeping beauty. That's good.

(Wilson kisses her.)

Mama? . . . Mama? . . . She's cold.

ADDISON: Jesus, you don't suppose she could be dead?

WILSON *(Startled)*: What?

ADDISON: I said, "Jesus, you don't suppose she could be *dead?*" Yup, that's how it looks. Well, what the hell. How'd you put it? You had a good phrase. "Face to the future, Brother! Good-bye to all that!"

WILSON: You crazy bastard—

(Wilson lunges at Addison.)

ADDISON *(Grabbing a knife off Mama's tray)*: Get out. *Get the fuck out!*

(A beat.)

WILSON: Goodness, would you look at the time. I'm afraid you'll have to excuse me . . . We may not see each other for some time. A kiss before parting, Brother?

(He steps toward Addison, puts a hand on the back of his neck. Addison shoves him viciously away. A Real-Estate Agent appears.)

REAL-ESTATE AGENT:
    Land boom!
    With a double whammy, boy!
    Land boom!
    Profits this thick!
    Land boom!
    Down around Miami, boy—

The weather's kinda clammy,
But it's get rich quick!

Brand-new communities,
Just take your pick.
Lots of opportunities—
All you need is capital,
A little does the trick.
Beg or steal or borrow,
It'll double by tomorrow.
Only get your ass to Florida
And get rich quick!

(The bed has been transformed into a railway compartment. In it sits the Handsome Young Man from the opening number. Addison enters, carrying a suitcase and a rolled-up set of architect's plans.)

HANDSOME YOUNG MAN: Excuse me, but I'd prefer to have this compartment to myself.

ADDISON: So would I, but the train is full.

(Addison sits, looks at the young man appraisingly. A beat.)

HANDSOME YOUNG MAN: What?

ADDISON: I was wondering if I should smile and introduce myself or just shut the fuck up?

HANDSOME YOUNG MAN: I'm sorry. Please, forgive me. I'm not usually . . . I haven't slept, that's all—

ADDISON: Addison Mizner.

HANDSOME YOUNG MAN: Hollis Bessemer.

ADDISON: That seemed to go all right. Shall we quit while we're ahead or try a little small talk?

HOLLIS: To tell the truth—

ADDISON: Where are you headed?

HOLLIS: Florida.

ADDISON: Uh-oh. Competition!

HOLLIS: I'm sorry?

ADDISON: I'm off to Miami to make my fortune. I wouldn't want anybody making theirs ahead of me.

HOLLIS: No, of course you wouldn't. Well, may you make your fortune, may you make *ten* fortunes, and may your riches bring you happiness—although if I were you, I damn well wouldn't count on it!

ADDISON: On second thought, maybe I will just shut the fuck up.

HOLLIS: Bessemer. Does that name mean anything to you?

ADDISON: It might if I saw it on the side of a blast furnace—

HOLLIS: My grandfather, he invented it. My father perfected it. Made millions from it. Expected me to help him make millions more. Unfortunately, commerce, industry, don't interest me. I told him that a thousand times. Told him again last night.

(Train sounds decelerating.)

We're stopping. Why are we stopping?

ADDISON: Can't see. It's probably—

HOLLIS: I can't afford to be delayed!

ADDISON: I'm sure it's just—

HOLLIS: You don't understand! He's cut me off! No allowance! No inheritance! Not so much as a penny! It's happened before, of course, but not like this. I have an aunt. Two hours before the train left I found out she was stopping in Palm Beach.

ADDISON: Palm Beach?

HOLLIS: Tiny town, middle of nowhere. Nothing there but a monstrosity of a hotel. She's looking for a place to build a house.

ADDISON: Really? A house?

HOLLIS: I sent her a telegram, begged her to wait for me—

ADDISON: Friendly refuge till the storm clouds clear, eh?

HOLLIS: It's more than that. I need her help.

ADDISON: With what? If you'd rather not . . .

HOLLIS: No, no, I'll tell you.

When I was a tyke,
I said, "What I like
Is art.
I know I'm a boy,
But what I enjoy
Is art."

Looking at paintings, going to plays,
Music and books informing my days,
Filling my mind,
Flooding my heart
With art!

I had this dream of becoming an artist—
A painter, a poet, who knows?
I had a nice little talent for drawing,
And a natural feeling for prose.
I even began to compose.

So many talents,
Wasn't I blessed!
All of them good,
A few of them better,
None of them best,

Just enough talent to know
That I hadn't the talent.
So I put my dream
And my self-esteem
To rest.

ADDISON: That must have been difficult.
HOLLIS: Yes. But it didn't matter. I merely had to find out what
I was meant to be.

ROAD SHOW

I couldn't decide,
Then one day I spied
Palm Beach.
A speck on the map,
No more than a gap—
Palm Beach.

Jungle and seashore, muddy and raw,
But in a flash I suddenly saw
What it would take,
What I could make
Palm Beach!

I had this dream of a city of artists,
Versailles by the Florida sea.
A sort of world congregation of artists,
All encouraged to set themselves free.
I knew what I wanted to be!

I'd be their host and supporter,
The patron saint
Of the things that they write
And compose and paint.

I shall wander among them with lavish praise
As they carve their statues,
Construct their plays,
Design their buildings,
Recite their rhymes,
Making modern art
Fit for modern times!

So many talents,
Gathered en masse!
Painters and poets,
Artists and dreamers,
Watered like grass.

And if the talent I have
Is for nurturing talent,
Then succeed or fail,
I will see they sail
First class.
And my father can go stick it up his ass.

(Palm Beach. Sounds of the sea. Edward and Eva Stotesbury on the veranda of the hotel.)

Aunt Eva, Uncle Edward—

MRS. STOTESBURY: Oh, hello, Hollis—

MR. STOTESBURY: Hello, boy. Eva said you might be turning up—

HOLLIS: I'm relieved to find you here. I was afraid you might have checked out.

MR. STOTESBURY: Leaving this afternoon.

MRS. STOTESBURY: Fleeing is more like it. *(For the benefit of a passing waiter)* This is a *very bad hotel.*

HOLLIS: Well: I assume you got my telegram.

MRS. STOTESBURY: Your telegram?

HOLLIS: About the artists' colony.

MRS. STOTESBURY: The artists'—? Oh, that. Hollis, honestly, I don't know where you get these outlandish notions.

HOLLIS: *Aunt Eva*—

MRS. STOTESBURY: You know, your father sent me a telegram, too. I didn't know Western Union *printed* words like that.

MR. STOTESBURY: Sounds like you've torn it this time, boy!

HOLLIS: Aunt Eva, Uncle Edward, *please.* He's cut me off without a cent! This colony means everything to me! Please, I need your help!

MRS. STOTESBURY: I need a house.

HOLLIS: You have three houses!

MR. STOTESBURY: Sophie Wanamaker has four.

ADDISON *(Joining the group)*: But Sophie Wanamaker hasn't got anything that looks like *this.*

(He unfurls his plans. Hollis stares at him.)

MRS. STOTESBURY: Excuse me, who are you?

HOLLIS: This is—

ADDISON: Addison Mizner. I'm an architect, in business with your nephew. He told me you wanted a house and here it is!

MRS. STOTESBURY: Hollis, you didn't—

ADDISON: He wanted to surprise you. Have a look. Please—

(The Stotesburys peer at the plans.)

MRS. STOTESBURY: Goodness, I've never seen a house like this before.

ADDISON: I should hope not! Echoes of Guatemala, a touch of the British Raj—

MRS. STOTESBURY: What's this bit? It's peculiar.

ADDISON: Well, I think every house should have a history, don't you? I imagined this one as an ancient castle on the coast of Spain . . . One stormy night it's overrun by Saracen invaders. They tear down the battlements, blow up the armory, and add a master bedroom suite with bath and powder room here, and a cloister for tea dances and tables of bridge, here. Next come the Goths, demolishing the dungeons and replacing them with ballrooms and a billiard room. They add a Venetian loggia up here and are pondering a breakfast nook, when who appears? The Moors! Raping and pillaging, and putting in cabanas and a tennis court before they're routed by the last invader—me—who adds an orangery, a servant's wing, and tops the whole thing off with Spanish tiles and the odd parrot. That's the peculiar bit. The parrot.

MRS. STOTESBURY: Edward, give this man money. He's building us a house.

ADDISON: Where?

MRS. STOTESBURY: Where?

MR. STOTESBURY: Well, I suppose it might as well be here. Hollis knows the town. He'll help us find a piece of property—

ADDISON: On the beach!

MRS. STOTESBURY: The beach.

HOLLIS: Would you excuse us for a moment? *(Taking Addison aside)* What in God's name is this about?! We aren't in business! I'm not interested in building houses! I want to build an artists' colony!

ADDISON: Look—
> Never let a chance go by, Hollis—
> Don't you see that here's your chance?
> How to stoke the fire
> Is the problem in acquiring a patron.
> Every patron has a matron.
>
> Let her feel fulfilled.
> Trust me, she'll be thrilled
> Once she sees the house that I'm going to build!
> And you'll get your guild.

HOLLIS: Aunt Eva, Uncle Edward, allow me to introduce you to your new house . . .

(The Stotesburys' Palm Beach mansion appears.)

MRS. STOTESBURY:
> Look at it!
> Look at it! Look at it!

Hollis, darling, you may put me at the head of the list of sponsors for your artists' colony. You may even name the administration building—the Eva and Edward Stotesbury Building. If Mr. Mizner will design it, of course.

ADDISON: Just as soon as my schedule permits.

HOLLIS:
> You . . .
> Where have you been all my life?

MRS. STOTESBURY:
    Look at it!

MR. STOTESBURY:
    Look at it!

MR. AND MRS. STOTESBURY:
    Look at it!

HOLLIS:
    You . . .
    You're the answer to my prayers.

MRS. STOTESBURY: Notice the details . . .

HOLLIS:
    You . . .
    You're one in a million.

MR. STOTESBURY: What's that? It's enormous!
ADDISON: Remember the breakfast nook?

HOLLIS:
    You . . .
    Where have you been all my life?

MRS. STOTESBURY: Wait till Edith Trumbauer sees it.
HOLLIS: About that administration building—

   (*Another pair of millionaires, Mr. and Mrs. Horace Trumbauer,
   appears.*)

MRS. TRUMBAUER: Hollis Bessemer!
HOLLIS: Hello, Edith.
MRS. TRUMBAUER: Where's this Michelangelo you found for
    your Aunt Eva?

HOLLIS: Edith Trumbauer, Addison Mizner.

MRS. TRUMBAUER: Mr. Mizner, the house you built for Eva is a work of art. You must build me one exactly like it.

ADDISON: No.

MRS. TRUMBAUER: No?

ADDISON: No, it has to be something for *you*.

> I see cypress arches, mosaic floors
> Reminiscent of the conquistadors,
> I see colonnades
> In a hundred shades,
> With a Roman cloister to house the maids,
> I see:

(The Trumbauer mansion appears.)

MRS. TRUMBAUER: Lovely . . . Isn't it?

ADDISON:
> You . . .
> You're the answer to my prayers.

MRS. TRUMBAUER: Lovely. Absolutely lovely.

ADDISON:
> You . . .
> You're one in a million.

HOLLIS: Edith, I'm sure Aunt Eva's told you about this artists' colony I'm cooking up—

MRS. TRUMBAUER: Yes, yes. But why is mine smaller than hers?

HOLLIS: That's merely the west wing . . .

(The Trumbauer mansion is now larger than the Stotesburys'.)

ADDISON:
> You . . .

HOLLIS:
> You . . .

ADDISON AND HOLLIS:
> Where have you been all my life?

HOLLIS:
> You . . .

ADDISON:
> You . . .

HOLLIS:
> You have the vision—

ADDISON:
> They have the money—

HOLLIS:
> We—

ADDISON:
> We—

ADDISON AND HOLLIS:
> Both have a dream.

HOLLIS:
> Me,
> I'd say we're a team.

ADDISON:
> Me, too.

ADDISON AND HOLLIS:
> Who knew that you'd come into my life?
> Where have you been?

(Mr. and Mrs. Joshua Cosden appear.)

MRS. COSDEN: Hollis Bessemer!

HOLLIS: Lily Cosden! I know—say hello to Addie Mizner.

MRS. COSDEN: My Joshua is being very naughty, Addie. He insists on giving me one of your handsome houses for my birthday.

ADDISON: When is your birthday?

MRS. COSDEN: March tenth.

ADDISON: Can't be done.

MR. COSDEN: Money is no object.

ADDISON: I'll see what I can do.

MRS. COSDEN: Make it like Edith Trumbauer's. Only in blue.

ADDISON:
Blue is for Norwegians, dearie,
Blue is not you.

MRS. COSDEN: No?

ADDISON:
No, you're a hacienda, a happy fusion
Of Indonesian and Andalusian—
I see gingerbread,
I see Chinese red
And a huge Victorian potting shed—

MRS. COSDEN: Fine, fine, just as long as it's finished by March tenth.

ADDISON:
(Under his breath:)
And a pond where you can go soak your head . . .

HOLLIS: Happy birthday!

ROAD SHOW

(The Cosden mansion appears.)

MR. AND MS. COSDEN:
>Look at it!
>Look at it!

MRS. STOTESBURY:
>Look at it!
>Their house has a view of the ocean, Addie,
>*And* such a view of the ocean!—

HOLLIS:
>Yes, but yours has the acreage . . .
>Yours has the privacy . . .
>Yours has the cupola—

MRS. STOTESBURY:
>The cupola? —

HOLLIS:
>The cupola that Addie's just designed for you—
>Looking down on the Cosdens'
>And out at the ocean . . .

MRS. STOTESBURY:
>Down on the Cosdens' . . .

HOLLIS:
>And out at the ocean . . .

ADDISON:
>You!—

HOLLIS:
>You!—

(More couples appear.)

MRS. WANAMAKER:
    Yoo-hoo, Mr. Mizner,
    A house for me . . .

HOLLIS: Addie, Sophie Wanamaker . . .

MR. DUPONT:
    And one for me!

MR. PHIPPS:
    We'll take two . . .

MR. DUPONT:
    Make that three . . .

HOLLIS:	MRS. WANAMAKER:
A house for Mr. Dupont!	Pardon me, but I was next.
A house for Mrs. Wanamaker!	MR. DUPONT: Don't be ridiculous.
ADDISON: I see minarets . . .	MRS. WANAMAKER: Alfred, tell her I was next.
I see parapets . . .	MR. WANAMAKER: She's next.
I see gargoyles . . .	MRS. PHIPPS: It happens to be *our* turn!
HOLLIS: A house for Mrs. Phipps!	

ADDISON:

> Grottoes . . .

HOLLIS:

> Another house for Mrs. Phipps!—

MRS. COSDEN:

> A house for me!

HUSBANDS:

> A house for us!

WIVES:

> A house for them!

HUSBANDS:

> A house for me!

WIVES:

> Us!

HUSBANDS:

> Them!

HUSBANDS AND WIVES:

> Us!
> Ahhh . . .

(Papa appears.)

PAPA: My God, what a spectacle. Yammering featherheads, desperate to outdo each other in boorish ostentation! My boy, you have a *gift*! Don't let—

ADDISON: Papa? Get lost.

ADDISON AND HOLLIS:
    You, where have you been
    All my life?

    You, you're the answer
    To my prayers.

    We, we'll make a
    Paradise here.

HUSBANDS AND WIVES:
    You, where have you been
    All our lives?

    You, you're the answer
    To our prayers.

    You,
    You're one in a million . . .

ADDISON:
    And with your permission—

HOLLIS:
    And your ambition—

ADDISON AND HOLLIS:
    And their tradition
    Of acquisition,
    We'll build

ALL:
    A place
    Where a brand-new world can play.
    Where have you been all my life?
    Don't go away!

MRS. STOTESBURY:
    Yes, but theirs has a floating gazebo . . .

(A tropical night. Hollis and Addison at home.)

HOLLIS:
    First there's cocktails at the Cosdens'—

ADDISON: Oh, Jesus . . .

HOLLIS:
> Hon, we've got fish to fry.

ADDISON: Why don't you do this one without me?

HOLLIS:
> Then there's dinner at the Dodges',
> The reception at the Roosevelts'—

ADDISON:
> I think I'm going to die.

HOLLIS:
> And every party filled
> With millionaires who want to build
> The biggest villas since the days of ancient Rome.
> So what do you say
> We just stay
> Home?

ADDISON:
> You are the best thing that ever has happened to me,
> You are.
> *(Hollis waves him away, blushing)*
> Okay then,
> One of the best things that's happened to me,
> You are.

> They say we all find love—
> I never bought it.
> I never thought it
> Would happen to me.
> Who could foresee?

You are the goddamnedest thing that has happened to me,
Ever.
When did I have this much happiness happen to me?
Never.

I can't believe my luck,
And all I can do
Is be the best thing that's happened to you.

HOLLIS:

So what do you say
We just stay home?
What do you say we just go
Out on the boat and get smashed
And make love on the beach
And stare up at the moon?—

ADDISON: Holly . . .

HOLLIS:

You might just be the best thing that has happened to me,
So far.
Of course not much ever really has happened to me,
So far.

I didn't much like love,
I always fought it.
I never thought it
Would happen like this.

ADDISON:

Give us a kiss.

ADDISON AND HOLLIS:

We may just be the best thing that has happened to us—

ADDISON:

    Kiddo . . .

HOLLIS:

    Partner . . .

ADDISON:

    Another moment like this may not happen to us—

ADDISON:

    Partner . . .

HOLLIS:

    Lover . . .

ADDISON AND HOLLIS:

    When all is said and done,
    I have to agree:
    You are the best thing that's happened to me.

HOLLIS:

    Who knew?

ADDISON:

    Who dreamed?

ADDISON AND HOLLIS:

    Beats me.

    (Addison snorts a line of cocaine. Lights down on Hollis. Thunder. Wilson appears. He is in bad shape.)

WILSON: Hello, Brother.
ADDISON: And hel-lo, Willie. Well, what brings you to Palm Beach?

WILSON: Freight trains for the most part. Though the yard bulls pitched me off the last one in Jacksonville. From there, I walked.

(Wilson coughs.)

Well, I guess this is a surprise?

ADDISON: Not at all. I knew you'd turn up sooner or later. You don't look good.

WILSON: You do.

ADDISON: Sunshine and money!

(Wilson coughs again. Addison offers him a humidor.)

Cigar? . . . They're Cuban. Lady Astor sends 'em over faster than I can burn 'em up. Well: What can I do for you?

WILSON: I've been reading about you, in the papers—

ADDISON: There's a switch.

WILSON: They say you've got a partner. They meant a business partner, but I saw the photos—

ADDISON: Cut the crap and tell me what you want.

WILSON: I want to help you.

ADDISON: Yeah? I made a half a million bucks last month. You crawled in here spitting blood. What could you possibly do to help me?

WILSON: I've got an idea—

ADDISON: You mean you've got a *scheme*.

WILSON: I can help you, Addie. Honestly—

ADDISON: *Honestly?* When did you ever help anybody *honestly?*

WILSON: Okay, maybe I deserved that, but you're a businessman now, Addie, just like me—

ADDISON: Just like you, huh?

WILSON: All I'm saying is, sometimes in business you have to stretch the truth a little bit, you know that now—

ADDISON: You know what else I know? That in the end, no matter how much I "stretch the truth," the suckers *I* hook get

good value. They get a great, big, beautiful house. What did
anybody ever get from you besides a couple of cheap laughs,
a hangover and an IOU?

WILSON: Addie, listen—

ADDISON: Tell you what. If I decide to build a whorehouse or a
saloon, I'll call you. Until then—

WILSON: *Listen . . .*

> One day up, the next day down,
> That's the way it goes.
> One week you can own the town—
> Next week, hey, who knows?
> You and me, though, Brother mine, we're pros.

> The whole thing's nothing more than just a game.
> And what we both are good at is the game.
> Believe me, I'm not asking for
> Forgiveness—all the same,
> I'm asking to get back into the game.

> Given up booze, given up coke,
> Given up girls, don't even smoke.
> Got a bad break and wound up broke,
> Jesus, my life is one sad joke . . .

(Pause. Addison just stares at him.)

> Want me to beg? Want me to crawl?
> Want an apology? Your call.
> I was a prick, but after all,
> Jesus, I'm your brother!

(Another pause. Wilson sings with increasing desperation:)

> It's more than just the money that's at stake.
> It's even more than begging for a break.

75

Joke or not, it's my life!
If you want to twist the knife,
Then twist the knife . . .

Only please—!

(Wilson tilts forward and collapses.)

ADDISON: It won't work, Willie . . . Up and at 'em . . . Willie?

(Wilson doesn't move.)

Shit.

(Thunder. The following morning.)

SERVANT: We heard about your brother, sir. How is he?
ADDISON: The doctor says he's going to live.
SERVANT: That must be a great relief, sir.
ADDISON: I'm getting a second opinion.

(Hollis appears.)

HOLLIS: I have just had the most extraordinary conversation with
     your brother! He's got the most marvelous idea—
ADDISON: Every idea my brother's ever had has been a marvelous
     idea.
HOLLIS: Look, he was quite frank with me. I understand the two
     of you aren't on the best of terms—
ADDISON: Best of terms? Last time I saw him I tried to stab him.
HOLLIS: All right, all right, but listen. He wasn't trying to per-
     suade me, just describe this notion that he has, and I have
     to tell you, it sounded, well, to me it sounded . . .

(Wilson joins Hollis.)

ADDISON: Marvelous?

HOLLIS: Yes.

ADDISON: You've got an idea. What is it?

WILSON: Okay, straight to the meat, huh? Well, we all know that dozens of new cities are going up all over Florida, right? Delray Beach. Fort Myers. Fulford-by-the-Sea. What's the one thing they have in common?

HOLLIS: They're all vulgar, tasteless eyesores!

WILSON: Right. Unlike the exquisite residence in which we now sit, a residence designed by the most celebrated architect, not just in Florida, but maybe—

ADDISON: You're wasting your time, Willie. I'm not interested in building cities.

WILSON: No? Why not?

ADDISON: For one thing, I've already built one.

WILSON: Palm Beach? This isn't a city, it's a country club.

ADDISON: And for another, there are projects I'm considering that I actually care about.

WILSON: Like, for example—an artists' colony for Hollis . . .

HOLLIS:

> That's what I wanted, a city for artists,
> Versailles by the Florida sea.
> A kind of haven for hundreds of artists,
> Whose great patron saint would be me!
> And then I meet Willie and he
> Says to me,
> "Look what Addie's done,
> And he's just begun!
> Why be saint to hundreds?
> Be saint to one!
> Think what he can do!"
> Think what *we* can do,
> Willie, me and you!

ADDISON: "Willie"?

HOLLIS:

And you . . .
You'll design a city, Addie,
Like no city ever seen before.
Think of it: a city, Addie,
Every single window, every door—
You could build a Paris, Addie,
But Paris made anew,
A Paris for today.

WILSON:

Paris, USA—

HOLLIS:

A Paris made by you—
Addison's city!

WILSON:

Venice and jazz combined—

HOLLIS:

Addison's city!

WILSON:

Every last stick and stone designed
By the same screwy brilliant mind—

HOLLIS AND WILSON:

Addison's city!

HOLLIS:

Newport with fizz—

WILSON:

Rio with shade—

HOLLIS:

>Capri as it is,
>But not so staid.

WILSON:

>Not so much a city—a parade!

HOLLIS AND WILSON:

>Addison's city!

WILSON:

>The time is now,
>The place is now,
>Your chance to do what you
>Were born to do
>Is now.
>
>A chance like this will never come again,
>Believe me,
>Embrace it now.
>
>The moment's now.
>The door is wide,
>An opportunity
>That mustn't be
>Denied.
>Don't muff it now.

HOLLIS: What do you think?

ADDISON: I think my brother would say anything to get what he
wants.

WILSON: Forget about what I want, what do *you* want?

ADDISON: Look around, Willie. Did it ever occur to you that
I already have everything I want right now?

WILSON: And how 'bout what you used to want? You saw it all,
remember? "Office buildings, concert halls and railway sta-

tions! It's like there's a whole new way America should look
and it's all up here, between these ears!" You found your
road, Addie, you were heading down it. You just took a
wrong turn . . .

>   You should build a city, Addie,
>   Not just fancy forts for rich old farts.

HOLLIS:

>   Much more than a city, Addie,
>   More like an amalgam of the arts.
>   Something international but bold—

WILSON:

>   Everything too much.

HOLLIS:

>   European verve—

WILSON:

>   New York City nerve—

HOLLIS:

>   Only with the Mizner touch—

HOLLIS AND WILSON:

>   Addison's city!

HOLLIS: Don't you see? It really *is* a marvelous idea!
ADDISON: *Was*, maybe—
WILSON: But not anymore, is that it?
ADDISON: You make choices and you live with them.
WILSON: Nuts! This is the Land of Opportunities! And that
    includes the opportunity to start over. You didn't like who
    you were, so you made yourself over into someone else.
    Swell. Now it's time for another change. Time to be the

somebody you were going to be before you decided to be *me*
. . . when you're on the right road and you take a wrong turn,
sometimes it's a good idea to check the map—

HOLLIS *(Unfurling a map)*: Boca Raton.

ADDISON: English translation: "The Mouth of the Rat."

WILSON: A thousand acres of prime, undeveloped real estate
wrapped around an inlet up the coast. It just came on the
market. It won't be on the market long. And it's a perfect fit
. . . One investor . . . One promoter . . . And one artistic
genius with a vision that could change the world.

> You make it up—
> *(To Hollis:)*
> You make it real.
> Leave it to me to make the spiel.
> Everyone gets to spin the wheel!

ADDISON: And what else do you get?

WILSON:

> A chance for now
> To make amends,
> A chance to ditch the blues
> And pay my dues
> To friends.
> And if I chance to make a buck or two
> Along the way, and so do you,
> Why not?

HOLLIS: *Why not?* A blank canvas, Addie. Waiting for you to fill
it up . . .

WILSON:

> Oh, come on, Addie—
> The three of us together, what fun!

HOLLIS: Say yes!

WILSON:

> You and me against the world, Brother,
> You and me against the world!
> You and me together,
> But in very different weather—
> Now it's pretty.

HOLLIS AND WILSON:

> Don't you want to build a city?

ADDISON:

> All right, okay!

HOLLIS AND WILSON:

> The time is now,
> The place is here,
> This is the chance to open up a new frontier,

HOLLIS, WILSON AND ADDISON:

> And if there ever was a time to pioneer—

(The Company joins them. The Boca Raton promotion begins.)

ALL:

> The time is now!

WILSON: So:

GROUP OF WOMEN:

> Boca Ratone!
> You've got a charm all your own!

WILSON: Not "tone,"
ADDISON: "ton."

WILSON AND ADDISON: So:

GROUP OF MEN:
> Boca Raton!
> You've got so much going on!

WILSON AND ADDISON: Better.

ALL:
> It's where everyone goes,
> It's where everyone's gone,
> The spot that's hot
> Is Boca Raton!

(Addison settles at a drafting table and goes to work.)

HOLLIS: Well, I know what Addie's going to do, and I've got a rough idea what *you're* going to do, but what about me?

WILSON: You closed on the land, right?

HOLLIS: It's all ours, paid in full.

WILSON: The promotional account?

HOLLIS: Fully funded.

WILSON: Line of credit?

HOLLIS: Set up for any one of our three signatures.

WILSON: Then, kid, here's your next assignment: Sit back, relax and watch the Mizner Brothers go to work!

(An ON AIR sign lights up. Fanfare, the sound of a crowing cock.)

(Into a microphone) Good morning, America! It's time to wake up to tomorrow! Time to wake up to opportunity! Time to wake up to the life of luxury and leisure, which beckons to you from the golden shores of Boca Raton, Florida! Yes, friends, Boca Raton. First came Coral Gables, then Winter Haven, then Hollywood-by-the-Sea. But now, my friends, now comes the most magnificent piece of real

estate to hit the market since the Good Lord foreclosed on the Garden of Eden. Now, my friends, comes . . . *Boca Raton*! And here to tell you about it is our very own Boca Girl!

BOCA GIRL:

> Boca Raton,
> Come down to Boca Raton,
> Where every sky's the bluest you've seen,
> Where all year long the grass remains green
> And every beach is clean and pristine.

THE WOMEN:

> Buy a lot
> Or even two.
> Have we got
> A lot for you!

BOCA GIRL:

> Boca Raton,
> Come down to Boca Raton,
> Where every vista sparkles and gleams,
> City beautiful of your dreams!

THE COMPANY:

> The city beautiful,
> A work of art in itself.
> The city beautiful
> Could be displayed on a shelf.
>
> A picture-perfect place,
> A place of grace and space,
> A world of seaside sports
> And leafy malls,
> A world of jai alai courts
> And concert halls,

A world of boating, hot springs,
Golf links, tennis—
Newport, Saratoga, Venice . . .

THE MEN IN THE COMPANY:
Boca Raton—

THE WOMEN IN THE COMPANY:
You'll covet—

THE MEN:
Boca Raton!

THE WOMEN:
You'll love it!

ALL:

Best, though, not to delay!

THE WOMEN:
Come and see
The new frontier!

THE MEN:
Come and be
A pioneer!

THE COMPANY:
You'll agree
Tomorrow's here
Today
In Boca Raton!

ADDISON: How 'bout this? "Boca Raton! Where the Gulf Stream
bends Westward to caress the beach of each and every oceanfront lot!"

WILSON: Not "lot," "estate."

WILSON AND ADDISON: "Oceanfront estate."

HOLLIS: Is that true?

ADDISON: Is what true?

HOLLIS: That the Gulf Stream actually touches the shore at Boca Raton?

WILSON: Who knows? Is Maxwell House really good to the last drop?

ADDISON: Will Listerine really get you the girl?

HOLLIS: Advertising, yes, of course. I just think we want to keep these claims fairly general, that's all, so they don't come back to bite us—

WILSON AND ADDISON: Absolutely!

THE COMPANY:
> Take a boat or a bus,
> Come by road or by river—
> Throw your bags in a flivver
> Or take the sunshine express
> To your new address:
>
> Boca Raton,
> Come down to Boca Raton . . .

WILSON (*Into the microphone again*): Wilson Mizner again, friends, issuing an invitation. Put your feet up, close your eyes, and join me on a VIP tour of Paradise! There it is, rising up before us like the Emerald City of the legendary Oz himself—the shining Shangri-la of the New World . . .

THE MEN:
> Boca Raton,
> Come down to Boca Raton,
> Where everybody's wearing a smile,
> Where everybody's living in style,
> 'Cause everybody's making a pile.

THE WOMEN:

>Don't think twice,
>Take our advice:
>Get your slice
>Of paradise.

THE COMPANY:

>Boca Raton,
>Come down to Boca Raton,
>Where you can swim and mingle and play
>And invest in the USA!

AN EXCITED MAN: I'm rich! I'm rich! Look at it! Gold! Jewels!—

WILSON: Pardon me, friend, but I'm on the air here.

AN EXCITED MAN: I'm rich, I tell you! Look!

WILSON: Hang on a minute. Those aren't—?

AN EXCITED MAN: Doubloons! Pieces of eight! I bought a beach-front lot in Boca Raton, stuck my umbrella in the sand, and there it was! Who knows which lot may contain the next pirate chest?!

WILSON: Who knows, indeed. But, you know, when you bought that lot, you purchased something far more valuable than pirate treasure.

AN EXCITED MAN: I did?

WILSON: Friends, let me ask you something. What is America? A location on a map? A cherished way of life? Freedom? Liberty? Justice for all? We hold these truths to be self-evident, all right. They *are* America. But this— *(Displaying the dirt on his hands from the sides of the chest)* This is America, too—

HOLLIS: What in God's name are the two of you doing?

ADDISON: Selling sand to the Arabs.

HOLLIS: You aren't selling anything to anyone. He's lying to them! Buried treasure! Pieces of eight! And what's all this nonsense about *America*?

WILSON: You've heard the expression "land of opportunity"? Well, this is it. The land itself! Up in the Klondike we shoveled it aside to get at the wealth which it contained. Down here, it *is* the wealth! God bless America, my friends. 'Cause you can buy it. You can sell it. And it can make you rich . . .

(A Housewife–Type steps up to the microphone:)

HOUSEWIFE-TYPE: My name is Mary Monahan. The day the sales office opened in Boca Raton, I bought myself a lot for seven hundred dollars. Last week I sold it for seven *thousand.*

THE COMPANY:
    Gold!

BOOKKEEPER-TYPE: My name is Winthrop Tippet. A month ago I bought a piece of property in Boca Raton for two thousand dollars. Yesterday I sold it for five times that.

THE COMPANY:
    Gold!

FARMER'S WIFE-TYPE: My name is Ethel Mudd. Last month my Bert and I bought a lot in Boca Raton with our life's savings of eight thousand dollars. This morning we were offered ninety thousand for that lot and do you know what we said:

THE COMPANY: *No!*

    Buy it now,
    Sell it later
    And get rich quick!

    Pick a spot,
    Buy a plot,
    When the spot gets hot,
    Sell the lot.
    My friends, you know what

You just got?
You got really rich
Really quick!

Bound to make a bundle!
Sure thing!
Bound to make a bundle,
Just a matter of time . . .

HOLLIS: *Addie—*

THE COMPANY:

Just a matter of time . . .

ADDISON: What can I do for you, Holly?
HOLLIS: What can you do for me? Are you *listening* to this? Do
you—?
ADDISON *(Cutting him off)*: Correct me if I'm wrong, Holly, but
this whole thing was your idea, wasn't it? Don't want to lose
your nerve now.
HOLLIS: Lose my *nerve?* . . .

THE COMPANY:

(Simultaneously, under the above:)
Buy today,
Sell tomorrow,
And get rich quick!
Don't delay,
Beg or borrow,
Or come what may,
To your sorrow
You'll rue the day
That you didn't say,
"I want to get rich quick!"

Can't you hear the knocking?
Hear that sound?

What is that that's knocking
All around?
That's opportunity knocking!
Every property's prime
And the views are sublime
And the values just climb
And climb
And climb and climb and climb . . .

HOLLIS *(Indicating a sheet of paper that Wilson is holding)*: Excuse me, if you don't mind, I'd like to have a look at that.
WILSON: At what?
HOLLIS: Your next speech.
WILSON: Ah, ah! That would spoil the surprise!
HOLLIS: I just need to look at what you're going to say.
WILSON: The only thing you need to look at is that sales thermometer. And unless you want to say, "Thank you, Mr. Mizner," then I suggest you stop wasting my time.
HOLLIS: And I suggest you let me—

(Wilson shoves him. Hollis stumbles and goes down. For a moment, everything stops.)

ADDISON: Holly! Willie! What happened?!
WILSON: Your playmate's starting to cramp my style.
HOLLIS: Look at his eyes. Whiskey and cocaine.
WILSON: Help him up. I want to knock him down again.
ADDISON: Stop it, both of you!
HOLLIS: *Both* of us?
ADDISON: Willie, listen, we all know you're doing a terrific job, but you've been doing it practically nonstop. Maybe it would make sense if you took a break and—

(The ON AIR sign lights up. Wilson grabs the microphone. As he speaks the sound of a crowd rises behind him.)

WILSON: My friends, let me describe to you a road. It is a road like no other in the world. Two hundred feet in width, it boasts no less than twenty lanes for traffic. Ranks of royal palms, three deep, describe its borders. At night it is illuminated, not by vulgar streetlights, but by the soft glow of theatrical spotlights embedded in its marble curbstones. Down its center runs a sparkling waterway, a replica in every detail of Venice's Grand Canal. Like its namesake, it is adorned with ornate landings, opulent rialtos, and gondolas poled by genuine Italian gondoliers. My friends, much as it may sound like one, this road is no dream. It actually exists, or soon will. And as you gaze in awe upon its wonders, ask yourself this: What is life? I say it is a journey. A road down which we travel, ever seeking, never satisfied. An endless quest for something different, something better. Onward we go, restlessly reinventing ourselves. Searching for something that already lies before us. For in America, the journey *is* the destination! Or it has been, until now. Until tonight. Because the road which I have just described to you will take us someplace so spectacular that finally we can cease our searching, stop our wandering and be content. Where does it lead? To journey's end. Behold, my friends, Boca Raton!

HOLLIS: Addie, we have to end this.

ADDISON: Too late for that—

HOLLIS: No! We can stop him! But I need your help—

ADDISON: I think maybe you've had enough of my kind of help. Now leave me alone, I've got a building I'd like to finish . . .

(Hollis stares at him, then turns away. He looks at the radio.)

HOLLIS'S VOICE *(From out of the radio)*: Ladies and gentlemen, this is Hollis Bessemer speaking. It has come to my attention that the real-estate development at Boca Raton, Florida, with which I have heretofore been associated, is being promoted in a deceptive, dishonest and fraudulent manner. As a result, I have this day divested myself of all my

holdings and interests in Boca Raton. I would advise anyone who owns property there to sell it immediately. I would
advise anyone looking at property there to buy elsewhere.

WILSON: I really wish you hadn't done that, kiddo. I really do—

(An ear-splitting crash!)

Addison's City . . .

HOLLIS: *Addison's City?* This wasn't about *"Addison's City"*! About
art or architecture, about some vision in your brother's head!
This wasn't about *Addison* at all!

WILSON: No? Well, it sure as hell is going to be about Addison
now. You ruined him.

HOLLIS: *I* ruined him?! This started out as a legitimate real-estate
enterprise! A legitimate opportunity for a brilliant artist to
create his greatest art! You're the one who turned it into
some kind of a cocaine-fueled *con game*!

WILSON: Cocaine-fueled *con game*? Well, that's a little harsh.
Wouldn't you say that's a little harsh, Addie?

ADDISON: I don't know—

HOLLIS: You don't *know*?

ADDISON: I mean, yes, of course I know—I knew.

HOLLIS: You knew . . . You know, I think you did. From the
moment he showed up, I think you saw this coming, the
whole thing. He was your *brother*, for Christ's sake.

WILSON: Correction: I *am* his brother, for Christ's sake.

HOLLIS: Yes, you are. Which made me what? Your *mark*?

ADDISON: Stop it—

HOLLIS: No, no. 'Cause in the end, that's the only way this thing
makes sense, if it was something the two of you cooked up
together.

ADDISON: Holly—

HOLLIS: From that first moment on the train. Find the rich kid!
Fleece the rich kid! "Oh, Holly, you're the best thing that ever
has happened to me, you are." Did he script that for you? Did
the two of you rehearse it? Did he make a good *me*—?

ADDISON: *No!* No, credit where credit is due. You were the mark, all right. But you weren't *our* mark, Holly. You were *mine.* All mine. I wish I could say I bribed the porter to put me in your compartment, but that was just a stroke of luck. And what a stroke of luck it was! There you were, poor little rich boy—so sensitive, so misunderstood—so desperate to stick it to your big, bad capitalist daddy that you'd do anything to help the starving artists of the world. Well, you sure as hell helped this one, kiddo. I got rich, I got famous—and boy oh boy, did I get laid.

(Hollis slaps him, hard.)

HOLLIS: You have each other. You deserve each other.

(Hollis exits.)

WILSON: Addie, I'm sorry. I know how hard that was for you. I only—

ADDISON:
> *(Suddenly, exploding:)*
> Get out of my life!
> Get the hell out of my life!
> Whatever this race we're in,
> Okay, you win,
> It's done.
> And now that you've won,
> Get out of my life!
>
> It used to be fun
> To watch you scheme,
> And even be a part of it—
> At the start of it.
> It used to be fun to stand and beam
> At my brother, who was so fucking smart.

I thought we could go from scheme to dream,
But then
I thought we were a team.
Amen,
No more,
I've looked at the score:

You owe me a life,
A life of my own.
I wanted to glide like you—
Before I do,
Please—
Leave me alone.

Get out of my life,
So I can live it . . .
Just . . .
Go away.

WILSON: What if I did? I'd still be here.

You don't want me to go.
Come on,
You don't want me to go.
You may think, yes, you do,
Right now—
That's now,
But it just isn't so.

ADDISON: Go away, Willie. Please.

WILSON:
You see only what's wrong,
Not me,
I see two of a kind.
I see two who are way ahead,

Who've always read
Each other's mind.

And this isn't the end of the trip.
No, it's just the reverse.
Face it, Brother, we're joined at the hip.
And that is our curse,
And that is the miracle!

You don't want me to go.

ADDISON: Willie—

WILSON:
　　　Admit you don't want me to go.

ADDISON: Willie, yes I do, damn it.

WILSON:
　　　Though I'm not worth a lot,
　　　I'm what you've got,
　　　Which you'll never outgrow.

　　　We were stuck from "hello,"
　　　It was bound to explode.
　　　Don't you see we're the same,
　　　That whatever the game,
　　　This was always our road?

ADDISON:
　　　Stop it, Willie, enough.

WILSON:
　　　Come on, Addie, you love me!
　　　Come on, say it out loud!
　　　Come on, Addie,

You love me, you love me,
You've always been—!

ADDISON:

> All right, yes!
> I love you, I always have loved you!
> Does that make us even?
> Does that make you happy?
>
> And I want you to go.
> *(Beat)*
> And, no,
> I don't want you to go . . .

(Addison returns to the bed in which we first discovered him. Wilson exits.)

A WOMAN: Mr. Mizner. There's a gentleman to see you.

(Addison leans forward, then falls back on the pillows, as he did at the start. The door of a packing crate falls open, the same one that fell open before, revealing Wilson.)

ADDISON: Hello, Willie.

WILSON: They told me you were dead.

ADDISON: I am.

WILSON: Then that must mean . . .

ADDISON: Face down in a double Bourbon in a booth at the Brown Derby.

WILSON: Damn! And when I think of all the famous last words I'd rehearsed—

ADDISON: Show's over, Willie. I'm the only audience you've got left.

WILSON: You know what? It's a relief.

ADDISON: Hard times, huh?

WILSON: Hollywood! You know, I actually wrote a couple of pictures.

ADDISON: Did you really?

WILSON: Well, I was in the room when a couple of pictures got written.

(The vamp of "Waste" begins.)

    By the way, what'd *you* die of?

ADDISON: I got lonely.

WILSON: Yeah.

ADDISON: And, in the end, I guess I was ashamed.

WILSON: *Ashamed?*

ADDISON: I had a talent, Willie. I threw it away.

WILSON *(Climbing into bed with him)*: Nah . . . Well, yeah.

> Still, you got rich.
> Still, you got laid.
> Not such a waste.

> Only one hitch:
> Me, I'm afraid.
> Still, you were embraced.

ADDISON: It wasn't enough, Willie. It was also too much.

WILSON:
> So you fell short
> Of your dream—
> Come on, sport,
> We're still a team,
> We're made the same way—

ADDISON:
> So you say—

(Papa appears.)

PAPA: Boys, boys—
ADDISON: Oh, shit.
PAPA: A doting father's dying words, boys . . .

> There's a road straight ahead,
> There's a century beginning.
> There's a land of opportunity and more . . .

I expected you'd make history, boys. Instead, you made a mess.
WILSON *(As Papa fades away)*: A *mess*? What does he mean, "a mess"?
ADDISON: You know what he means.
WILSON: Yeah. Well. One man's mess is another man's . . . something or other.

ADDISON:

> God, you had charm,
> God, you had guts.
> God, what a waste.

WILSON: Hey! We built a city!
ADDISON: Actually, we didn't.

> God, we did harm.
> What, were we nuts?
> And, where was our taste?

WILSON: So we went overboard a little bit. Where's the harm in that?
ADDISON: Where's the *harm*—?

WILSON:

> So if we fell,
> And fell fast,
> Why should we dwell

On the past?
Looking ahead—

ADDISON:
Willie, we're dead.

WILSON: I know it's a long shot, but you don't suppose this could be Heaven, do you?
ADDISON: God keeps better books than that, Willie.
WILSON: Then where do you think guys like us go after they die?
ADDISON: I don't think they go anywhere. I think they just keep going . . .

(A chord plays, like the one that accompanied the appearance of Addison's first house in Palm Beach.)

THE COMPANY:
Look at it!
Look at it! Look at it!

(Addison and Wilson stare out over the heads of the audience.)

WILSON: Addie, look at it! You know what that is? It's the road to opportunity!
ADDISON: It's the road to eternity.
WILSON: The greatest opportunity of all. Sooner or later we're bound to get it right.

(Blackout.)

THE END

STEPHEN SONDHEIM wrote the music and lyrics for *Road Show* (1999–2009), *Passion* (1994), *Assassins* (1991), *Into the Woods* (1987), *Sunday in the Park with George* (1984), *Merrily We Roll Along* (1981), *Sweeney Todd* (1979), *Pacific Overtures* (1976), *The Frogs* (1974), *A Little Night Music* (1973), *Follies* (1971; revised in London, 1987; and in New York, 2001), *Company* (1970), *Anyone Can Whistle* (1964) and *A Funny Thing Happened on the Way to the Forum* (1962), as well as lyrics for *West Side Story* (1957), *Gypsy* (1959), *Do I Hear a Waltz?* (1965) and additional lyrics for *Candide* (1973). *Side by Side by Sondheim* (1976), *Marry Me a Little* (1981), *You're Gonna Love Tomorrow* (1983) and *Putting It Together* (1992, 2000) are anthologies of his work.

For film, he composed the scores of *Stavisky* (1974) and *Reds* (1981) and songs for *Dick Tracy* (Academy Award, 1990). He also wrote songs for the television production *Evening Primrose* (1966), co-authored the film *The Last of Sheila* (1973) and the play *Getting Away with Murder* (1996), and provided incidental music for the plays *The Girls of Summer* (1956), *Invitation to a March* (1961) and *Twigs* (1971). He won Tony awards for Best Score for a Musical for *Passion*, *Into the Woods*, *Sweeney Todd*, *A Little Night Music*, *Follies* and *Company*: all of these shows won the New York Drama Critics Circle Award as did *Pacific Overtures* and *Sunday in the Park with George*, the latter also receiving the Pulitzer Prize for Drama (1985).

Mr. Sondheim was born in 1930 and raised in New York City. He graduated from Williams College, winning the Hutchinson Prize for Music Composition, after which he studied theory and composition with Milton Babbitt. He is on the Council of the

Dramatists Guild, the national association of playwrights, composers and lyricists, having served as its president from 1973 to 1981, and in 1983 was elected to the American Academy of Arts and Letters. In 1990 he was appointed the first Visiting Professor of Contemporary Theatre at Oxford University, and in 1993 was a recipient of the Kennedy Center Honors.

JOHN WEIDMAN has written the books for a wide variety of musicals, including *Pacific Overtures* (Tony nomination, Best Book), *Assassins* (Tony Award, Best Musical Revival) and *Road Show* (Lucille Lortel nomination, Best Musical), all with scores by Stephen Sondheim; *Contact* (Tony nomination, Best Book; Tony Award, Best Musical), created with director/choreographer Susan Stroman; *Happiness,* score by Scott Frankel and Michael Korie, directed and choreographed by Susan Stroman; *Take Flight* and *Big* (Tony nomination, Best Book), scores by Richard Maltby, Jr., and David Shire; and the new book, co-authored with Timothy Crouse, for the Lincoln Center Theater revival of Cole Porter's *Anything Goes* (Tony Award, Best Musical Revival; Olivier Award, Best Musical Production). Since his children were pre-schoolers, Weidman has written for *Sesame Street,* receiving more than a dozen Emmy awards for Outstanding Writing for a Children's Program. He is a graduate of Harvard College and Yale Law School, and from 1999 to 2009 he served as President of the Dramatists Guild of America.